CARROLL SCHOCHLER PRIMARY SCHOOL

MIGHTY MOVERS

Dump Trucks

A Buddy Book
by
Sarah Tieck

ABDO
Publishing Company

VISIT US AT

www.abdopub.com

Published by ABDO Publishing Company, 4940 Viking Drive, Edina, Minnesota 55435.

Copyright © 2005 by Abdo Consulting Group, Inc. International copyrights reserved in all countries. No part of this book may be reproduced in any form without written permission from the publisher. Buddy Books™ is a trademark and logo of ABDO Publishing Company.

Printed in the United States.

Written and Edited by: Sarah Tieck
Contributing Editor: Michael P. Goecke
Graphic Design: Maria Hosley
Image Research: Sarah Tieck
Photographs: Corbis, Michael P. Goecke, Photos.com

Library of Congress Cataloging-in-Publication Data

Tieck, Sarah, 1976-
  Dump trucks / Sarah Tieck.
     p. cm. — (Mighty movers)
  Includes index.
  ISBN 1-59197-825-4
     1. Dump trucks—Juvenile literature. I. Title.

TL230.15.T54 2004
629.225—dc22

                       2004050235

Table of Contents

What Is A Dump Truck?

A dump truck is a large truck. Dump trucks help move things. They carry dirt, snow, rocks, and other things.

The back of the dump truck is called a bed. This is where the dump truck carries its load.

The dump truck's bed lifts up and dumps out the load.

Dump Truck Parts

Dump truck bed

S·100

Hydraulics lift the bed.

Special cover gives the operator extra protection.

Cab

Inside the cab.

Large mirrors help the driver see behind the truck.

Gauges help the driver.

What Do Dump Trucks Do?

Dump trucks work at construction sites and mines. A dump truck is a building machine. Dump trucks help get land ready for building.

At a construction site, some building machines dig holes. Other building machines clear trees and rocks from the land. This makes the land ready for building.

A dump truck unloads dirt at a construction site.

The building machines load the dirt, rocks, and branches into the back of the dump truck. The dump truck moves the dirt, rocks, and branches to another place.

Dump trucks also help make roads. Dump trucks move dirt and rocks. They also bring the supplies to make the road's surface.

Dump trucks help build roads.

Loading A Dump Truck

Many building machines load dump trucks at a construction site.

Front-end loaders

Front-end loaders are building machines. They have a big shovel on the front. Front-end loaders scoop up dirt. The big shovel drops dirt into dump truck beds.

A front-end loader fills the bed.

Excavators

Excavators are building machines. Excavators dig holes using a bucket. The bucket is like a shovel. The bucket lifts out rocks and dirt.

An excavator digs a hole.

Dump trucks work at construction sites with excavators, cranes, and other machines.

GIANT DUMP TRUCKS

Some dump trucks are as big as a house. They are too big to drive on the road with cars. These are giant dump trucks.

A giant dump truck can be 50 feet (15 m) long. A giant dump truck can measure 27 feet (8 m) wide and 24 feet (7 m) high. Giant dump trucks can weigh as much as 410,000 pounds (186,000 kg). Giant dump trucks can carry 620,000 pounds (281,200 kg).

How Dump Trucks Work

One crew member drives the dump truck. The driver is called the operator. The operator rides in the dump truck's cab. The cab is made to be safe. There is a special cover to protect the operator from rocks.

The driver uses levers to make the bed move. The levers make the dump truck work. The driver can move the levers to make the bed go up or down.

When the driver moves the levers, the bed lifts up.

Hydraulics

A dump truck's bed works because of something called hydraulics. Hydraulics is the use of liquids such as water and oil to move machines. Pressure created by the liquid makes the machine's parts move. Hydraulics help dump trucks move dirt.

How Hydraulics Work for a Dump Truck

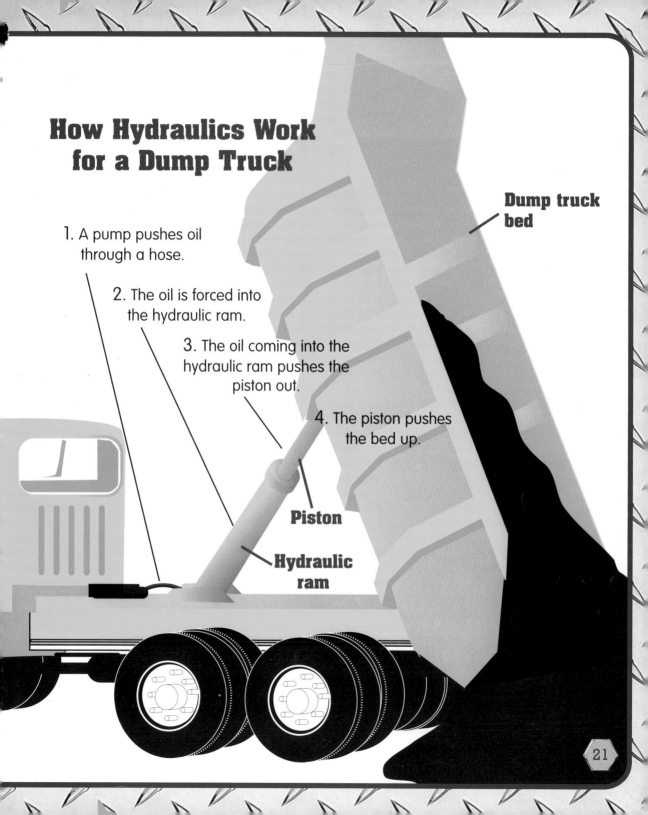

Dump truck bed

1. A pump pushes oil through a hose.

2. The oil is forced into the hydraulic ram.

3. The oil coming into the hydraulic ram pushes the piston out.

4. The piston pushes the bed up.

Piston

Hydraulic ram

The dump truck empties a load.

Important Words

construction site the place where a house or building is built.

crew a group of people who work together.

hydraulics the force of liquid, which is used to make machines move.

levers a bar that the operator moves to make the machine move.

operator the crew member who operates a building machine.

Web Sites

To learn more about dump trucks, visit ABDO Publishing Company on the World Wide Web. Web site links about dump trucks are featured on our Book Links page. These links are routinely monitored and updated to provide the most current information available.

www.abdopub.com

Index